CRICUT DESIGN SPACE:

The Ultimate Guide for Beginners and Advanced Users. Tools, Explore Air 2 and Design Space, Cricut Projects for all Levels, Tips & Tricks, Practical Examples and Much More.

JADE PAPER

CRICUT DESIGN SPACE

© **Copyright 2020 by Jade Paper - All rights reserved.**

The content contained within this book may not be reproduced, duplicated or transmitted without direct written permission from the author or the publisher.

Under no circumstances will any blame or legal responsibility be held against the publisher, or author, for any damages, reparation, or monetary loss due to the information contained within this book. Either directly or indirectly.

Legal Notice: This book is copyright protected. This book is only for personal use. You cannot amend, distribute, sell, use, quote or paraphrase any part, or the content within this book, without the consent of the author or publisher.

Disclaimer Notice: Please note the information contained within this document is for educational and entertainment purposes only. All effort has been executed to present accurate, up to date, and reliable, complete information. No warranties of any kind are declared or implied. Readers acknowledge that the author is not engaging in the rendering of legal, financial, medical or professional advice. The content within this book has been derived from various sources. Please consult a licensed professional before attempting any techniques outlined in this book.

By reading this document, the reader agrees that under no circumstances is the author responsible for any losses, direct or indirect, which are incurred as a result of the use of information contained within this document, including, but not limited to, — errors, omissions, or inaccuracies.

Table Of Contents

Introduction 6

Chapter 1: Machine Setup 14

Chapter 2: Cricut Explore Air And Design Space 22

Chapter 3: Projects Design For Beginners The Basic 28

Chapter 4: Tools In Cricut Design Space 38

Chapter 5: Intermediate And Advanced Level Projects 48

Chapter 6: Cut Vinyl With A Cricut Machine 74

Chapter 7: Selling And Make Money 84

Chapter 8: Cricut Design Space Top Menu 90

Chapter 9: Tips And Tricks And Hacks For Cricut Design Space. 100

Chapter 10: Cricut Design Space Vocabulary 108

Chapter 11: How To Edit And Upload Images In The Cricut Machine 116

Chapter 12: Slice, Flatten, Weld, Attach And Contour Info-Graphic Slice 134

Conclusion 138

Introduction

Cricut Design Space is the online stage that Cricut designed to be utilized with their more up to date machines. It's not programming – you download a module on your PC (or the application on your table/telephone), and after that, you can design however much you might want.

You can utilize designs and pictures that are now transferred into Design Space or you can transfer your own!

Cricut Design Space is 100% free. You do need to make a record; however, if you would prefer not to, you don't need to spend a penny.

Cricut Design Space is an online programming program that enables you to interface with your cutting machines by means of USB or Bluetooth. It's the way you make most of the wonderful designs that will wind up on your tasks, shirts, cushions, espresso cups, and the sky is the limit from there!

As an option in contrast to making your own designs or getting them from Cricut, I regularly shop at Etsy (simply scan what you're searching for with SVG toward the end) and afterward "play with" my designs.

While they have some free pictures and textual styles incorporated with the program, there are ones that you can pay cash for. You can likewise pursue a Cricut Access Plan, which will give you access to a great many pictures and textual styles.

Be that as it may, you can introduce your own textual styles onto your PC and transfer pictures to Design Space (that you've made, found for nothing, or obtained without anyone else).

Cricut Design Space is an online program, so you don't download it onto your PC.

Nonetheless, you should download some modules, which should auto popup and brief you to download when you experience the underlying procedure.

If you are needing to download Cricut Design Space onto your iPhone or iPad, then you will simply need to go to the Apple App Store, scan for "Design Space," and it ought to be the primary alternative to spring up. Download it like you regularly would.

Any undertaking that you make in Design Space can be spared to the Cloud. You simply need to ensure you spare your venture – which catch is in the upper right hand corner.

This enables you to see your task on any gadget where you are signed in. Nonetheless, if you are dealing with an iPhone or an iPad, you have the choice to spare it just to your gadget. I would, for the most part, consistently propose sparing it to the Cloud, however!

You can utilize Design Space on Mac PCs, PC PCs, and iOS gadgets.

Your PC must run a Windows or Mac working framework, and hence, Google Chromebooks CANNOT be utilized, as they keep running on a Google OS.

Once in a while when you go to cut your design, it will stop you before you at the tangle see page and state you have to pay.

You may have incidentally included a picture that requires installment – you can return to your canvas and check each picture to check whether there is a dollar sign beside it (or check whether the text style you chose has a dollar sign. Remember that regardless of whether you have Cricut Access, you don't approach ALL the pictures and textual styles).

If you chose a venture from Design Space, it might have incorporated a picture or textual style that is paid. When you take a gander at the task guidelines, it should let you know if it is free or not.

I see this inquiry all the time in Design Space, and it very well may be so disappointing! Frequently, Design Space is down when they are making refreshes.

Some of the time, they will convey an email when they anticipate a blackout. However, I don't generally observe this.

If it's down, I would propose not reaching their client backing and simply be quiet. You can likewise attempt another program or clear your program store, just to ensure it is anything but an issue on your end.

Cutting is one of my preferred highlights in Cricut Design Space! I cherish removing text styles and pictures in different designs. Yet, now and then it won't work. If you are observing this to be an issue, here are a couple of thoughts:

– Make sure the picture/text style you are removing of (so that is over another picture) is totally inside the other picture. If a bit of it is standing out, it won't cut.

– Make sure everything is chosen.

– Keep as a main priority that when you cut it, you will have two layers to expel from the picture – the first picture/text style that you cut, just as the cut

For what reason isn't print and cut working?

I won't jump a lot into Print and Cut, as it is a monster all alone.

Notwithstanding, the most compelling motivation why I see individuals experiencing difficulty with Print and Cut is that they didn't smooth their pictures! Before you go to print and cut, ensure you select all and press straighten.

For what reason Can't I Open Cricut Design Space?

Regularly you will get a blunder or a white screen with Design Space if you don't have the most as of late refreshed module.

If you get a clear page, take a stab at invigorating the page to check whether the module update shows up. Try not to move far from this page when it's refreshing, or it will turn white.

Cartridge

Designs are produced using parts put away on cartridges. Every cartridge accompanies a console overlay and guidance booklet. The plastic console overlay demonstrates key determinations for that cartridge as it were. Anyway, as of late Provo Craft has discharged an "All-inclusive Overlay" that is perfect with all cartridges discharged after August 1, 2013. The motivation behind the all-inclusive overlay is to simplify the way toward slicing by just learning one console overlay as opposed to learning the overlay for every individual cartridge. Designs can be removed on a PC with the Cricut Design Studio programming, on a USB associated Gypsy machine, or can be legitimately inputted on the Cricut machine utilizing the console overlay. There are two kinds of cartridges shape and textual style. Every cartridge has an assortment of imaginative highlights which can take into consideration several different cuts from only one cartridge. There are as of now more than 275 cartridges that are accessible (independently from the machine), containing textual styles and shapes, with new ones included monthly. All cartridges work just with Cricut programming, must be enrolled to a solitary client for use and can't be sold or given away. A cartridge obtained for a suspended machine is probably going to wind up futile at the point the machine is ended. Cricut maintains whatever authority is needed to suspend support for certain renditions of their product whenever, which can make a few cartridges quickly out of date.

The Cricut Craft Room programming empowers clients to join pictures from different cartridges, consolidate pictures, and stretch/turn pictures; it doesn't take into account the formation of discretionary designs. It additionally empowers the client to see the pictures showed on-screen before starting the cutting procedure so that the final product can be seen in advance.

Referring to Adobe's surrender of Flash, Cricut declared it would close Cricut Craft Room on 15 July 2018. Clients of "heritage" machines were offered a markdown to refresh to models good with Cricut Design Space. Starting at 16 July 2018, Design Space is the main programming accessible to make projects. Design Space isn't perfect with cartridges once in the past bought for the Cricut Mini, which was power nightfall in October 2018.

Third-party

Provo Craft has been effectively unfriendly to the utilization of outsider programming programs that could empower Cricut proprietors to remove designs and to utilize the machine without relying upon its exclusive cartridges. In a similar audit of bite, the dust cutting machines, survey site identified being "restricted to cutting designs from a gathering of cartridges" as a noteworthy downside of the Cricut run; however, the audit noticed that it could be an inclination for some.

Two projects which could once in the past be utilized to make and after that get Cricut machines to remove subjective designs (utilizing, for instance, self-assertive TrueType text styles or SVG group illustrations) were Make-the-Cut (MTC) and Craft Edge's Sure Cuts A Lot (SCAL). In April 2010 Provo Craft opened lawful activity against the distributers of Make-the-Cut, and in January 2011 it sued Craft Edge to stop the conveyance of the SCAL program. In the two cases, the distributers settled with Provo Craft and expelled support for Cricut from their items. The projects keep on being usable with other home cutters.

As indicated by the content of its lawful grumbling against Craft Edge, "Provo Craft utilizes different strategies to encode and cloud the USB correspondences between Cricut Design Studio [a design program provided with the hardware] and the Cricut e-shaper, so as to secure Provo Craft's restrictive programming and firmware, and to avoid endeavors to capture the cutting commands". Provo Craft battled that so as to comprehend and imitate this darkened convention, Craft Edge had dismantled the Design Studio program, in opposition to the provisions of its End User License Agreement, along these lines (the organization affirmed) breaking copyright law. Provo Craft additionally affirmed that Craft Edge was damaging its trademark in "Cricut" by saying that its product could work with Cricut machines. Provo Craft declared this was likely "to cause perplexity, misstep or double dealing with regards to the source or starting point of Defendant's merchandise or benefits, and [was] prone to erroneously recommend a sponsorship, association, permit, or relationship of Defendant's products and ventures with Provo Craft."

CHAPTER 1:

Machine Setup

Setting up your machine could look somehow complicated or tedious. However, this unit is majorly written to guide you through it; the unboxing process and the setting up. So, relax and bring that Cricut machine out wherever you've stashed it. It takes approximately 1 hour to finish setting up a Cricut machine. With this guide, you should be done in less than an hour. Let's get right on it, shall we?

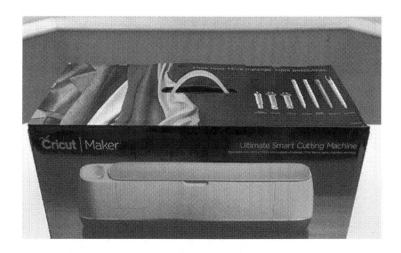

STEP 1: OPENING THE BOX

To make sure that we are together all the way through, we will go through even the most trivial step; opening the box.

You should be having a number of boxes right now in front of you if you went for the whole Cricut bundle. And there should be a big box among those boxes which contains the Cricut machine itself. If you open that big box, the first thing you should find is a Welcome packet; most of the tools will be in that packet. You should find a welcome manuscript, rotary blade and cover, a USB cable, a fine-point pen, a packet that contains your first die-cutting project. The USB cable is sometimes the last thing you'll see in this packet, it's hidden under every other stuff. Underneath this welcome packet is your Cricut machine.

To find the power cable, you first need to bring out the machine out from its box. You will then discover the power cable underneath the box with two cutting mats of standard sizes. That looked easy, right? Let's proceed to the following step.

STEP 2: UNWRAPPING YOUR CRICUT MACHINE AND SUPPLIES

We are getting to the exciting part. Let's unwrap your machine and find out what's inside.

When trying to unwrap your machine, you'll find it covered in a protective wrapper that looks filmy and also with a cellophane layer. Try to carefully unwrap the top foam layer so you can see the machine clearly. After that, go on to remove the remaining part of the Styrofoam that protects the inner machine housing.

When you unbox the whole casing, you should expect to find the following tools;

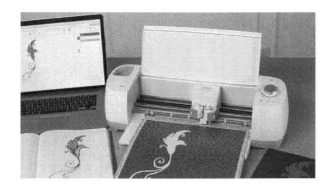

Cricut Machine

USB and Power Cables

Rotatory blade with housing.

Fine point blade with housing

Fine point pen.

Light-Grip and Fabric-Grip Mats (12 x 12)

STEP 3: SETTING UP YOUR MACHINE

Finally, we can move on to getting your machine up and running. Most of what you'll be doing will be technically inclined. You basically need electricity, a mobile phone or computer with internet access. Once you have access to all these, plug your power cord into an electronic outlet and then switch on your machine.

I'll assume your Cricut machine has Bluetooth function. If it does not have this function, either make use of the USB cable to connect your computer and the Cricut machine or purchase a Bluetooth adapter as soon as you can.

Once they are all connected, open your computer browser to continue the setup. Visit the Cricut Sign-in Page and click on the "Sign in" icon. You will have to either sign in with your account details or create a new account for yourself if you don't already have one. This is necessary so as to be able to access the Cricut Design Space.

If you do not have an active account yet, don't bother to fill any information on the sign-in fields. Click on the "Create Cricut ID" in the green box and then fill out every field with the required information and click on "Submit."

Create a Cricut ID

Your Cricut ID is your golden ticket to all things Cricut

[form: First Name, Last Name, Country, Email / Cricut ID, Retype Email / Cricut ID, Password, I accept the Cricut Terms of Use, Send me free inspiration & exclusive offers]

Already have a Cricut ID?
Sign In

Now, it's time to link your machine to your account. It takes some people a lot of time to finish this part successfully. To make it easier, follow the procedures below.

After signing in, go to the upper left corner of the page and click on the drop-down menu icon (with three lines) beside "Home."

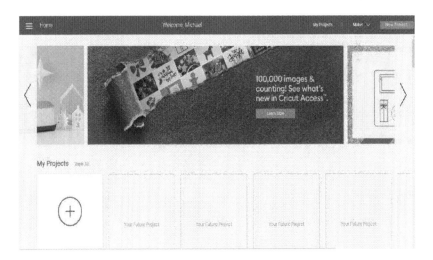

When the drop-down menu appears, select the "New Machine Setup."

On the following screen that pops up, click on your Cricut machine model.

Another webpage will appear with instructions on how to connect your machine. Follow the instruction accordingly.

When you follow the instructions, it automatically detects your machine and prompts you to download and install the software.

The site is user-friendly, so you'll be directed on how to go about the installation. And if you already have an account, you may still need to download it again. Cricut updates their design space often, there could be some new tools in the latest version that you don't have access to. It only takes about five minutes to get the installation done.

And there we go; we have concluded the setup procedure on your PC. That wasn't too hard, was it?

You might find the software a little bit complex for you when you first start to explore it. But with constant usage, you'll master it.

STEP 4: CLAIMING YOUR BONUS

When you have successfully created an active account on Cricut, you can claim access to Cricut for a whole month for free! It's a welcome bonus from Cricut. You'll have access to different projects, fonts, as well as Cut files. You can exploit this opportunity by making use of the accessible library to work on several fun projects.

STEP 5: COMMENCING YOUR FIRST PROJECT

You may want to start practicing with some old projects done by other people or study how they are done before you initiate your personal project. Every Cricut machine comes with a trivial project. You'll find it in the welcome pack. You can use this to get familiar with the tools the machine came with.

It may be challenging to make use of the Cricut Design Space without fully knowing its environment. So, stick with small projects till you get better, or ask someone who has more knowledge and experience with Cricut tools to guide you through.

CHAPTER 2:

Cricut Explore Air and Design Space

The Cricut Explore Air is the subsequent stage up from the Explore One. It also comes the standard Fine-Point Blade which enables you to cut several materials, and it's good with the Deep Point Blade and the Bonded Fabric Blade (sold independently) to enable you to cut considerably more materials.

One major redesign over the Explore One is that the Cricut Explore Air has a double apparatus holder; it is intended to hold a cutting edge in one clamp and a pen, scoring stylus, or another embellishment in the other clip. This implies if you have a project that has both writing and cutting, you can stack a sharp edge and a pen into the machine and it will cut and write across the board go without stopping for you to change between instruments. Far better, the second clasp is perfect with tools like the Scoring Stylus, Cricut Pens, and so on so there's no reason to buy an extra connector.

The Cricut Explore Air also offers worked in Bluetooth abilities. For the initial step, you should associate utilizing the USB link gave, yet after the underlying matching, you'll have the option to interface with your machine and cut remotely.

Features

- With double cartridge to cut, compose or score simultaneously
- With inserted Bluetooth, so you can work remotely
- Will cut in excess of 60 distinct materials
- With incorporated stockpiling segments
- Good with .svg, .jpg, .png, .bmp, .gif, .dxf documents
- Will take a shot at all Cricut cartridges

Pros

- Cut and compose, cut and score simultaneously
- You can work remotely
- Store pens, blades and different frill away compartments
- You can utilize your very own pictures or utilize any picture from the tremendous library
- Works with Cricut cartridges

Cons

- You have to buy extra apparatuses and accessories
- You have to buy fonts and designs

Cricut Explore One

The Cricut Explore One is Circuits' entrance level spending machine; it's ideal for any individual who needs to begin with a digital die cutting machine yet wouldn't like to spend a huge amount of cash. It accompanies the standard Fine-Point Blade which enables you to cut several materials, and it's perfect with the Deep Point Blade and the Bonded Fabric Blade (sold independently) to enable you to cut considerably more materials.

As its name suggests, the Explore One has a single apparatus holder, so if you need to cut and write in a similar project you should change out the sharp edge for a pen mid-route through the cut. It's extremely simple to change out the accessory or blade, and the Design Space programming will stop the slice and walk you through it when now is the right time, yet if you do a lot of tasks that join cutting, composing, or scoring, it can get tiresome sooner.

Moreover, really, the single tools holder is good with the standard estimated edges (Fine-Point, Deep Point, and Bonded Fabric), however to utilize different instruments and extras, you'll have to buy a different connector to fit in the single device holder.

The Explore One doesn't have worked in Bluetooth capacities, so you need to connect the machine to your gadget with the USB link gave. Or then again you can buy a Bluetooth connector independently to enable the machine to cut remotely.

Features

- Utilize the Cricut Design Space for PC, Mac, iPad or iPhone
- Transfer your own plans for nothing or pick one from the Cricut Image Library
- Use text styles introduced from your PC
- Work on various materials from flimsy paper to thick vinyl
- With helpful device and extras holder
- Works remotely by including a remote Bluetooth connector
- No compelling reason to set with the Smart Set dial or make your very own custom settings
- Make extends in minutes

Pros

- Works remotely with Bluetooth connector
- Transfer your very own pictures and structures for nothing
- With 50,000+ pictures and text styles from Cricut Image Library
- No settings required with the Smart Set dial
- Prints and cuts quick
- Structure with your very own gadget or PC utilizing Design Space

Cons

- It expenses to utilize pictures beginning at $0.99

- Bluetooth connector sold independently

CHAPTER 3:

Projects Design for Beginners the Basic

When starting a new project, you'll want to know what that project will be and what materials you will be using before doing anything else.

For example, if you want to cut vinyl letters to place on wood, you'll need to know all of your dimensions so your letters fit evenly and centered on the wood. You'll need wood that vinyl can adhere to without the risk of peeling. And you'll want to make certain that your wood is sanded and finished to your desire because you don't want any imperfections. You may find even with store-bought wood pieces advertised as ready-to-use, there are tiny imperfections.

You want to make sure when working with fabric that you know what inks or vinyls will adhere to the surface. You don't want any peeling or cracking to happen to your beautiful design.

When working with any kind of fabric, including canvas bags, you'll want to prewash for sizing because shrinkage after your design has been set can cause the design to become distorted.

If you aren't sure exactly what you want to do, have something in mind so that you aren't wasting a lot of materials by trial and error.

The cost of crafting materials can add up, so you'll want to eliminate as much potential waste as possible.

If you're new to Cricut Design Space, start with something simple. That's the worst thing you can do when you learn any new craft. There are many used Cricut machines for sale, and while some users sell because they upgraded, others are users who gave up. You made the investment and you'll want to get a return on that investment.

Project for Beginners

Leafy Garland

Garlands are an easy way to spruce up any space, and there is an infinite variety of them. Create a unique leafy one to give your home a more naturalistic feel! Feel free to change the colors of the leaves to suit you, whether you stick with green or go a little more unnatural. Tweaking the size of the bundles you make and how close you put them together will change the look of the garland. You can use different types of leaves as well. Experiment a little bit to see what you like best. Bending the leaves down the center and curling the edges a little will give you a more realistic look, or you can leave them flat for a handmade look. You can use the Cricut Explore One, Cricut Explore Air 2, or Cricut Maker for this project.

Supplies Needed

Cardstock – 2 or more colors of green, or white to paint yourself

Glue gun

Lightstick cutting mat

Weeding tool or pick

Floral wire

Floral tape

Instructions

Open Cricut Design Space and create a new project.

Select the "Image" button in the lower left-hand corner and search for "leaf collage."

Select the image of leaves and click "Insert."

Place your cardstock on the cutting mat.

Send the design to your Cricut.

Remove the outer edge of the paper, leaving the leaves on the mat.

Use a pick or scoring tool to score down the center of each leaf lightly.

Use your weeding tool or carefully pick to remove the leaves from the mat.

Gently bend each leaf at the scoreline.

Glue the leaves into bunches of two or three.

Cut a length of floral wire to your desired garland size, and wrap the ends with floral tape.

Attach the leaf bunches to the wire using the floral tape.

Continue attaching leaves until you have a garland of the size you want. Bundle lots of leaves for a really full look, or spread them out to be sparser.

Create hooks at the ends of the garland with floral wire.

Hang your beautiful leaf garland wherever you'd like!

Easy Envelope Addressing

Christmas cards are wonderful to send out, but they can take forever to address. Address labels just don't look as personal, though. Use the Cricut pen tool in your machine to "hand letter" your envelopes! You can use this for your batch of holiday cards or even for other cards or letters. This takes advantage of the writing function of your Cricut machine. For the most realistic written look, make sure you select a font in the writing style. It will still write other fonts, but it will only create an outline of them, which is a different look you could go for! Cricut offers a variety of Pen Tools, and there are some other pens that will fit as well. For addressing envelopes, stick to black or another color that is easy to read so that the mail makes it to its destination. You can use the Cricut Explore One, Cricut Explore Air 2, or Cricut Maker for this project.

Supplies Needed

Envelopes to address

Cricut Pen Tool

Lightstick cutting mat

Instructions

Open Cricut Design Space and create a new project.

Create a box the appropriate size for your envelopes.

Select the "Text" button in the lower left-hand corner.

Choose one handwriting font for a uniform look or different fonts for each line to mix it up.

Type your return address in the upper left-hand corner of the design.

Type the "to" address in the center of the design.

Insert your Cricut pen into the auxiliary holder of your Cricut, making sure it is secure.

Place your cardstock on the cutting mat.

Send the design to your Cricut.

Remove your envelope and repeat as needed.

Send out your "hand-lettered" envelopes!

Easy Lacey Dress

Lace dresses are adorable, but they can be hard to get ahold of and difficult to make. Fake it without anyone knowing better using your Cricut! The iron-on vinyl will look just like lace, and it will stand up to your child's activities much better than the real thing. Don't limit yourself to children's clothes; add some vinyl lace to your own as well! White vinyl will look like traditional lace the most, you can do this in any color that coordinates with the dress that you have. Use a Cricut EasyPress or iron to attach the vinyl to the fabric. You can use the

Cricut Explore One, Cricut Explore Air 2, or Cricut Maker for this project.

Supplies Needed

Dress of your choice

White heat transfer vinyl

Cricut EasyPress or iron

Cutting mat

Weeding tool or pick

Instructions

Open Cricut Design Space and create a new project.

Select the "Image" button in the lower left-hand corner and search "vintage lace border."

Choose your favorite lace border and click "Insert."

Place your vinyl on the cutting mat.

Send the design to your Cricut.

Use a weeding tool or pick to remove the excess vinyl from the design.

Place the design along the hem of the dress with the plastic side up. Add lace wherever you like, such as along the collar or sleeves.

Carefully iron on the design.

After cooling, peel away the plastic by rolling it.

Dress your child up in her adorable lacey dress!

Paw Print Socks

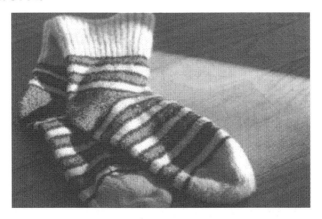

Socks are the ultimate cozy item. No warm pajamas are complete without a pair! Add a cute, hidden accent to the bottom of your or your child's socks with little paw prints. Show off your love for your pet or animals, in general, every time you cuddle up! You can do this with almost any small design or even use text to add a quote to the bottom of your feet. You can use any type of socks you find comfortable. For the easiest read, make sure the sock color and vinyl color contrast. Or, make them in the same color for a hidden design! The shine of the vinyl will stand out from the cloth in certain lights. Since this uses heat transfer vinyl, you'll need your Cricut EasyPress or iron. You can use the Cricut Explore One, Cricut Air 2, or Cricut Maker for this project.

Supplies Needed

Socks

Heat transfer vinyl

Cutting mat

Scrap cardboard

Weeding tool or pick

Cricut EasyPress or iron

Instructions

Open Cricut Design Space and create a new project.

Select the "Image" button in the lower left-hand corner and search "paw prints."

Select the paw prints of your choice and click "Insert."

Place the iron-on material on the mat.

Send the design to the Cricut.

Use the weeding tool or pick to remove excess material.

Remove the material from the mat.

Fit the scrap cardboard inside of the socks.

Place the iron-on material on the bottom of the socks.

> Use the EasyPress to adhere it to the iron-on material.
>
> After cooling, remove the cardboard from the socks.
>
> Wear your cute paw print socks!

CHAPTER 4:

Tools in Cricut Design Space

A cricut research machine may cut pretty much anything so long as it's 2.0mm thick or thinner. And in case you've got a cricut maker, that device has one0x the cutting force and also may cut stuff up to 2.4mm thick!

Cardstock and paper

The cricut is good at cutting paper and cardstock, but it does not only cut scrapbook paper!

Vinyl

One other fantastic substance the cricut machine may cut is vinyl. Vinyl is awesome for creating signs, stickers, stencils, images, etc...

Iron on vinyl, also called heat transport vinyl, is just one of my favorite substances to cut with my cricut! You are able to use iron vinyl to decorate t-shirts, tote bags, or some other cloth item.

- flocked iron about
- foil iron on
- glitter iron on

- glossy iron on
- holographic sparkle iron about
- matte iron on
- metallic iron on
- neon iron on
- printable iron on
- Fabrics and textiles

The cricut does a fantastic job at cutting edge fabrics, but you certainly need to add a stabilizer such as wonder beneath or heat'n bond prior to cutting. These cloths and fabrics can be trimmed using a cricut research machine, however you will find even more which it is possible to cut together with the rotary blade onto a cricut maker machine.

- burlap
- canvas
- cotton fabric
- denim
- duck fabric
- faux leather
- faux suede

- felt
- flannel
- leather
- linen
- metallic leather
- oil fabric
- polyester
- printable fabric
- silk
- wool felt

Additional materials

Besides cloth, paper, and vinyl, there are tons of additional specialization stuff a cricut can cut also.

Cricut maker

In case you've got the maker, then you are able to cut more stuff! The cricut maker has one0x the cutting edge force of the research machines; also it's a rotary blade along with a knife blade which let it cut more stuff. The cricut maker may cut stuff up to 2.4mm thick, and over one25+ kinds of cloth, such as:

- chiffon

- cashmere
- fleece
- jersey
- jute
- knits
- moleskin
- muslin
- seersucker
- terry cloth
- tulle
- tweed
- velvet
- Iron on vinyl

Iron on vinyl is mainly utilized on matters which are cloth based in certain way like t-shirts, bags, fabric scraps etc...

Iron on vinyl (a.k.a heat transport vinyl or htv) is an absolute favorite for many cricut users and functions nicely with a fine-point blade, however, what exactly are a few of the best iron on vinyls to utilize?

1. Cricut heat transfer vinyl -- cricut's vinyls are excellent as they're created for cricut and from cricut. They also offer you an enormous selection of shades and textures like glitter.

2. My vinyl immediate -- vinyl direct includes a good deal more than only htv, so I'll direct you back to it over once. They have loads of patterns, colors and textures to store!

3. Firefly heat transport vinyl -- firefly is a widely known and reliable manufacturer. Does it have good appraisals but they also have a great choice! And if you're seeking good fuzzy flocked vinyl or gloss vinyl they are you covered!

4. Fame heat transport vinyl -- this new is great once you're searching for a large choice of colors. Another advantage of this new brand is the fact that it's cheaper than some choices if you're on a budget!

Mat to utilize: normally the typical grip mat will operate with vinyls.

Adhesive vinyl -- use vinyl putting

Glue vinyl is a snug favorite into the htv. There are an infinite number of applications for glue vinyl like wall stickers, mugs, decorations, boxes, wall art etc... Below are a few of the greatest brands beneath for av!

There are basically two types of glue vinyl -- durable exterior and detachable indoor -- with numerous types within each class. Vinyl will continually be described among those types and also you ought to use accordingly to this job for the best results.

By way of example, removable adhesive vinyl could work good as a detachable wall decal while durable vinyl will function better to get a timber signal you intend to hang in your door.

For glue vinyl you will generally utilize the plastic placing on your own cricut.

1. Oracal vinyl -- this vinyl is my own top option once i am considering starting a glue plastic undertaking. Oracle is thought of as the market leader when it comes to craft vinyl. This vinyl is designed to last decades. You could even locate traces of the on vinyl direct here in either matte or polished!

2. Cricut adhesive vinyl -- cricut remains a fantastic go to source for av. As an entire cricut does are far pricey but there are times that i discover a much better color in a color I'm looking for using cricut's vinyl.

3. Expressions vinyl -- expressions vinyl is another popular and user friendly. They've a fantastic color choice of glitter too!

4. Joyful crafters -- frankly this is only a joyful place site -- you may discover vinyl of all kinds and several other craft related materials!

Mat to utilize: standard grip function as well for glue vinyl.

Cardstock

Paper and cardstock are close and dear to me since i like to create paper flowers. Actually, you can access my entire library of snacks when you register!

1. Recollections cardstock -- recollections is a new by Michael's craft store, but they could also be found on the internet! I use this particular brand the very best for my newspaper crafts.

2. Savage universal newspaper rolls -- I recently found just how wonderful savage paper functions for paper crafting. Though it sounds somewhat expensive upfront, it lasts a lot more!

3. Paper and much more -- paper and more is a trustworthy source I've used and I really like the unique colors that they have.

4. Cards and pockets -- this website was with me for many years and therefore, the color choices are unparalleled to many.

Mat to utilize for cardstock paper: standard grip

Added fine-point blade materials

Let us also cover additional substances that work together with the fine-point blade and also the standard grip mat:

Lean chipboard -- great for wreathes or big letter or number workouts. Establish dial to habit and choose chipboard.

Lean poster board -- utilize for jobs with wallpapers or large cut outs. Dial ought to be put to poster board.

Stencil sheets -- produce your own customer stencils along with your cricut! I have employed the cardstock setting for stencil substance but should you purchase a different brand which is thicker than 6 mil you will to go up on the strain.

Sticker newspaper or tattoo newspaper -- should you're using the cut and print attribute, look at doing it on tattoo or decal paper for an enjoyable undertaking. I love to reduce my planner decals! Utilize the cardstock setting for all these as well with the fine-point blade.

Vellum -- vellum is simply another kind of newspaper that's usually delicate and translucent. It works excellent for any variety of paper crafts. For vellum, be certain that you place the dial to vinyl or paper.

Cellophane -- each currently and I locate a job I'm generating needs a flexible and transparent like substance -- cellophane works good for this along with also your cricut can cut it! Cellophane will have to get cut in the lightest setting, typically the one dot before it.

Deep-cut blade -- which can I trim?

For all the substances below you will want to place your machine or dial to custom and research the title of the content to place the appropriate cut strain.

Chipboard -- should you will need a thicker chipboard then exactly what the fine-point blade can manage, and then place your deep cut blade to get the job done!

Rubber -- want to create your own stamps? You can with this fantastic rubber along with also the deep-cut blade.

Wood veneer antiques -- you could have the ability to use a fine-point blade together with the timber veneer if it's thin , but likely will need the profound blade ordinarily.

Magnets -- making your own magnets could be really enjoyable. A fantastic teacher appreciation present in reality.

Leather -- leather is the rage at this time, particularly those snazzy leather earrings!

Craft foam -- foam is particularly wonderful for children crafts. Pre-cut a lot of fun shapes and also have your children enjoy some catchy fun time!

Mat board -- mat board is essential cardboard however nicer. So any project that you would like to use cardboard can work together with the profound cut blade!

Felt sheets -- love sensed blossoms or crafts? Then let your cricut perform the job for you! You might also conduct stiffened sheets!

Glitter cardstock -- I really like my glitter cardstock to get a sorts of endeavors. I've cut it using the fine-point blade although the profound works especially with all the chunky glitter paper. Craft shops frequently have some or utilize the link I supplied!

Preferences: for the stuff in this segment you may probably choose habit for a lot of them and specify in design space which you are using on the trim display. Layout space includes a setting for these choices.

Fabric blade -- what do I cut?

The cloth blade is pretty unique to cloth and you'll generally keep the cloth setting set up on the dial. Listed below are a couple of my favorite fabric areas to store. You might also cut cloth using the two former blades i advise giving the cloth intended blade a go! Spoonflower -- if you want a good deal of cloth to select from or to custom design your own cloth in a few short clicks afterward spoonflower is your thing to do!

Joann fabrics -- most of you have likely heard of Joann's fabrics. They've been around quite a while and a number of you might have a shop nearby. If you do not, you can store here online!

Fabric immediate -- if you would like a significant website filled with cloth and at wholesale rates, then make sure you check out cloth direct. I've bought velvet from them for a few autumn pumpkin crafts and adored it!

Mat to utilize: fabric grip mat or regular grip.

Knife blade (cricut maker just) -- what do I cut?

Together with the knife blade (cricut maker just) you can cut a great deal of similar cricut substances as with the profound sword but the difference is that it may cut 2-3x thicker stuff then the research can deal with! Thick leather -- the knife blade was commended for how well and wash it cuts thicker leather substances. Therefore, in the occurrence that you would like to earn those stylish leather earrings or perhaps a clutch handbag then this really is exciting! Incidentally check out this golden and silver leather!

Thick chipboard -- should you desire a heftier chipboard material that the knife blade may take can of this.

CHAPTER 5:

Intermediate and Advanced Level Projects

When you begin to venture into the types of projects needing more expertise, you will find that you need to branch out to websites providing their own design and cutting files that you can use to create more and more imaginative stuff. For this reason, I would suggest searching for various online tools for projects you can do to expand your horizons when it comes to more complex projects! There's a list of 100 crafts you can do with your Cricut device to really make your crafts special to you to give you some ideas to get you started on where to look!

3D Wood Puzzles

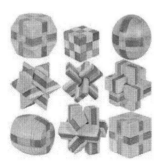

You may have seen these in the museum gift shops or in the brainy kids ' toy store unit. Both are incredibly fun and, when put together, they make for a fantastic final product.

3D Foam Puzzles

For 3D puzzles, foam is just as strong so you can take them apart, bring them back together, knock them down, and more, and they bounce back.

These make such a wonderful gift to young people.

3D Wall Art

Art that pops off the wall and gives a message to all the guests about who you are is something that people pay a lot of money to have. Put on your wall a little bit of your artistic self, and show off your imagination!

Aprons

If you're a kitchen enthusiast, your apron is a perfect way to add a customized touch to your experience. You can completely own the kitchen with a character that you love, a funny saying, or just a monogram.

Banners

Any occasion with a banner is more official! Using Cricut, you can use your resources to create a special banner that will remember the opportunity at hand beautifully.

Beanies

A knit cap is a perfect way to stay warm for any outdoor activity that's going to happen during the winter months. Getting one on the side emblazoned with your own logo is sure not only to elevate the hat style but also to make many wonders where they can get one like it!

Beer Steins

Sometimes, the dollar store may have blank glass beer mugs that literally call out to craftsmen to decorate them. Create a memorable gift in your life for the beer lover!

Bookmarks

Bookmarks are such an easy craft, but they are needed almost always! If your circle is like mine, everyone around you is still in the middle of reading a manuscript. Replace the supermarket receipt with something fun and personal in the center of their novel!

Bumper Stickers

There will still be something of a theme to greet the drivers behind you in traffic. Create some fun comments to put on a bumper for you and your mates.

Business Cards

It can be so costly to get business cards made from premium stock and in unusual shapes. Printing the designs using a regular printer on cardstock and cutting out complex designs are sure to catch the attention of potential clients.

Cake Toppers

Did you come up with a fun birthday party? Using plastic or metal to make a gorgeously decorated cake topper that will blow your guests away.

Calendars

No matter how the times advance, you must always know which day it is! See if you can make exclusive calendars for your desk or office!

Candles

Yeah, you can't make your Cricut candles yourself. But you could get a candle in a blank glass holder and put something Beautiful on the outside of it for any occasion. Let me tell you these make perfect gifts.

Canvas Tote Bags

Tote bags are among the Planet's most popular accessories. Keep all your things together, and add some Cricut style to it! Heck, you could get some canvas if you felt like it, and make your own tote bag!

Car Decals

Did you have a business? Tell that to the universe as you fly through your week!

Centerpieces

Any large-scale event could take advantage of themed centerpieces to entertain and wow your guests!

Clothing

Put your artistic flourish with Cricut and the various materials they have to give on something that you own. Whether it is an iron-on decal or an embellishment of a dress, there is no lack of ways to please.

Coasters

Like so many other stuffs on this list, coasters will make such a perfect housewarming or holiday gift. All should use a specific set of coasters to maintain safe and dry surfaces!

Coffee Mugs

Coffee mugs are probably the only dish in my house. I'll ever want more when I see them. They're great for so many things, and you're the ideal addition to every office or kitchen, having ones that are original.

Coloring Pages

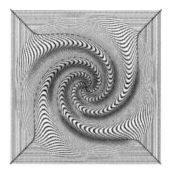

You can download line art using the pen on your Cricut to make coloring pages of any type or theme for yourself or your loved ones! If you have kids coming to visit your family, that makes for a great group activity!

Commemorative Plates

Do you know that materials from Cricut that can stick to ceramics could make a perfect decoration for commemorative plate decoration? What times do you remember?

Craft Foam Shape Sets. Much as with the puzzle sets, you can cut out craft foam just about any shape you like. Doing so with an adhesive backrest on the foam sheets will allow you to make your own little sewing sets of whatever themes you want! This requires letters too!

Decorative Plaques

Just as you saw in the segment on Cricut Projects for Beginners, decorative plaques are a breeze, and you will become more detailed and artistic as you acquire more experience with the Cricut method.

DIY Craft Kits

Creating the Cricut parts for crafting kits is a breeze. Let your imagination run wild on what bits you should put together to create your own design ideas for others! Let your judgments run rough on this one as they make perfect party favors, children's or crafts gifts, and so much more!

DIY Decals

You may put the decals you make on a carrier or backing sheet to be given out. If you don't want to put your decal right on it, simply top up with a transfer tape piece and give it away!

Doilies

Cricut's intricate designs allow you to create doilies with so many different fabrics, colors, sizes, shapes, themes, and more!

Envelopes

Were you aware that envelopes are made of one continuous piece of paper that is simply cut, folded, and glued in a particular way? This means you can take any piece of paper you want, print whatever you want, and make an envelope from it! Go crazy. Go crazy.

Flowerpots

A flower pot can be a kind of worldly object. However, they can turn into something that perfectly suits your decor with some craft paint and a stencil that you made with your Cricut, or with a decal!

Framed Affirmations

This is a difficult life! Affirmations you can put in your own font or style will make all the difference from a personal space in the vibe you receive. Jazz up your own and put it all over your house!

Gift Card Envelopes

It can really be achieved with scrapbooking paper, construction paper, foil paper, or whatever. You can turn this tiny little gift into something that everyone would love to have, very personal.

Gift Tags

As you've seen in the segment on Cricut Projects for Beginners, these tags can take on any simple gift and give it such imaginative pop. Going the little bit extra for making someone look like a gift and feeling special really makes a difference.

Greeting Cards

Many of the supermarket's most beautiful greeting cards will cost you about $9 a card these days! You can make cards that are just stunning, multi-layered, with the materials to hand in at your carving station and make them bear your personal message. It makes the whole gift so personalized and meaningful.

Hats

There are designs for making your own hats, and you can also make decals that will make an existing hat pop!

Holiday Décor

I can't even be frank about how crazy I have been in this group. There are so many decorations you can make for every event that you really can't even imagine doing them all for a holiday!

Hoodies

Perhaps nothing is more convenient than a sexy, thick hoodie. Put your own personal touch on a hoodie, or bring your favorite characters or phrases around the label.

Jewelry

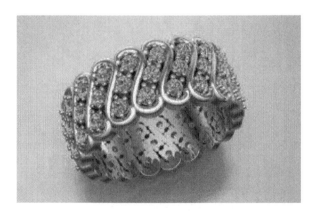

Oh right. With the products available through Cricut, you can totally make your own jewelry. Leather, cloth, metal. There is everything.

Keepsake Boxes

Any art is full if it cannot be connected back to hold sake boxes in some way, right? They are all over the crafting world, and you can make boxes for keepsake or simply decorate them to the nines.

Key Fobs

Make your keys stand out by making an adorable or stylish fey fob!

Keychains

Got a favorite character or emoji? Make a keychain!

Labeled Kitchenware.

From canisters to kitchen crocks, there's nothing you can't decal!

Labels

If organizing is your weapon, using Cricut will help you make beautiful labels for every room in the house!

Lanyards

Keep your keys or ID cards displayed with style and comfort.

Leather Accents

Leather accessories can also elevate your designs from looking fantastic to look fully professional, from scrapbooking to home décor.

Leather Accessories

Wrist bands, belts, lanyards, cash clips, etc. Your Cricut will turn leather sheets into your prettiest, most stylish accessories.

Luggage Tags

Just rest assured which bag you are on the carousel. Design as much as you can a luggage tag that stands out from the crowd and claim your bag in no time!

Magnetic Poetry Sets

You can produce a series of magnetic poems and limericks on your doors, fridges, or metal tables by printing words onto a collection of printable magnets!

Magnetic Puzzles

Puzzles are an ever-enjoyable timeless gift. Print a loved one's image onto a printable magnet, make a jigsaw puzzle, and build a beautiful package for your front refrigerator or a friend!

Magnetic Storytelling Sets

You can build a series of magnetic stories and jokes on your doors, fridges, or metal tables by printing words onto a collection of printable magnets!

Magnets

Think outside the box and make your own magnetic designs, then cut them into unique shapes to place your own style on your fridge or door.

Makeup Bags

Customizing a basic zippered bag will make the item all the difference in style! Call them. Yours! You might even use your Cricut to make your own zippered bag, and then decorate it!

Mandala Decals

Mandalas are amazing, and Cricut is the ideal device to help you make decals to put on about anything.

Mason Jars

Mason jars are perfect for anything from drinking to decoration, so with this one, the sky is the limit! See what exclusive things you might put on yours.

Monogram Decals

Render it with monograms on all of your accessories very uniquely.

Name Plates

Crafter in Hand. Crafter Extraordinaire, Caren Smith. The Big Cheese. If you want people on your desk or workplace to see, it can happen!

CHAPTER 6:

Cut Vinyl with a Cricut Machine

Vinyl is self-evident, and kid did I have NO clue that there was such a significant number of. I have kept my utilization of vinyl entirely basic as of not long ago, just utilizing regular classic vinyl. However, I can't hold back to give a shot such a significant number of these vinyl choices underneath.

You can likewise utilize the Deep Cut Blade for thick cardstock and cardboards.

- Adhesive Vinyl
- Chalkboard Vinyl
- Dry Erase Vinyl
- Glitter Vinyl
- Metallic Vinyl
- Outdoor Vinyl
- Printable Vinyl
- Stencil Vinyl

- Glossy Vinyl

- Holographic Vinyl

- Matte Vinyl

The Best Materials for Cricut Explore and Maker

Iron-on vinyl

Iron-on vinyl is transcendently utilized on things that are fabric situated somehow or another, for example, shirts, totes, cloth napkins and so on.

For iron-on vinyl make certain to utilize the iron-on setting on your Cricut.

Iron-on vinyl (a.m. heat transfer vinyl or HTV) is a flat out most loved for most Cricut clients and functions admirably with a fine-point sharp blade, however, what are a portion of the absolute best iron-on vinyl to utilize?

Siser Heat Transfer Vinyl – Easy to weed and they have been around for quite a while! Siser likewise has sparkle vinyl alternatives, patterned vinyl, and floral patterns just as holographic choices!

My Vinyl Direct – Vinyl Direct has much progressively then just HTV. They have a lot of examples, colors, and surfaces.

Firefly Heat Transfer Vinyl – Firefly is broadly known and confided in the brand. In addition to the fact that it has extraordinary appraisals, they have a phenomenal determination! What's more, if you are searching for extraordinary fluffy flocked vinyl or glitter vinyl they have you secured!

Fame Heat Transfer Vinyl – This brand is incredible when you are chasing for a wide choice of colors. The other advantage of this brand is that it is less expensive than a few other options if you are on a spending limit!

MAT to utilize: Generally the standard hold mat will work with all vinyl.

Adhesive Vinyl – Use Vinyl Setting

Adhesive vinyl is a nearby most loved to the HTV. There are endless uses for adhesive vinyl, for example, decals, mugs, decorations, compartments, divider craftsmanship and so forth. Here are probably the best marks beneath for AV!

There are fundamentally 2 classifications of adhesive vinyl – changeless open-air and removable indoor – with different kinds inside every category. Vinyl will consistently be explained as one of those sorts and you should utilize in like manner to the undertaking for best outcomes.

For instance, removable adhesive vinyl would work extraordinary as a removable wall decal while lasting vinyl will work better for a wood sign you intend to hold tight your front entryway.

For adhesive vinyl, you will generally utilize the vinyl setting on your Cricut.

Oracal Vinyl – This vinyl is my own top decision when I am considering starting an adhesive vinyl project. Oracal is viewed as the industry leader with regards to craft vinyl. This vinyl is intended a year ago. You can likewise discover moves of this on Vinyl Direct here in both gleaming and matte!

Cricut Adhesive Vinyl – Cricut is as yet an extraordinary go-to resource for AV. All in all, Cricut tends to be increasingly expensive BUT there are times that I locate a superior conceal in a shading I am checking for with Cricut's vinyl.

4. Happy Crafters – Honestly this is only an upbeat place site – you will discover vinyl of various kinds and numerous other art-related supplies!

Mat to utilize: Standard hold fill in also for adhesive vinyl.

Cardstock

Paper and cardstock are used to make paper flowers

1. Recollections cardstock – Recollections is a brand by Michael's craft store, however, they can likewise be discovered online! Utilize this brand the most for my paper creates.

2. Savage Universal paper rolls – I recently found how brilliant Savage paper functions for paper creating. Even though it appears to be a little expensive forthright, it endures so any longer!

3. Paper and More – Paper and more is a believed resource I have utilized and I love the more one of a kind colors they have.

4. Cards and Pockets – This site has been with me for a considerable length of time and in light of current circumstances, the color alternatives are unrivaled to most.

Thin chipboard – useful for wreaths or large letter or number patterns. Set dial to custom and select chipboard.

Thin poster board – use for projects with foundations or huge patterns. Dial ought to be set to the poster board.

Sticker paper or tattoo paper – If you are utilizing the print and cut component, consider doing it on sticker or tattoo paper for a fun project. I like to cut my own organizer stickers! Utilize the cardstock setting for these also with the fine-point blade.

Vellum – Vellum is simply one more sort of paper that is typically sensitive and translucent. It works extraordinary for any variety of paper makes. For vellum, try to set the dial to paper or vinyl.

Cellophane – Every from time to time I discover a task I am making needs an adaptable and clear like material – cellophane works incredible for that and your Cricut can cut it! Cellophane should be cut at the lightest setting, typically paper or the one speck before it.

Deep-cut blade – What Can I cut?

For every one of the materials underneath you will need to set you dial or machine to custom and search the name of the material to set the proper cut pressure.

Elastic – Want to make your very own stamps? You thoroughly can with this extraordinary elastic and the deep-cut blade.

Wood veneer embellishments – You may have the option to utilize a fine-point blade with the wood veneer if it is slim enough, however likely will need the deep blade in most cases.

Magnets – Creating your very own magnets can be extremely fun. An astounding teacher thankfulness blessing actually.

Leather – Leather is extremely popular at this moment, particularly those sweet leather earrings!

Craft foam – Foam is particularly great for children's crafts. Pre-cut a lot of fun shapes and have your children appreciate some crafty fun time!

Matboard – Matboard is a basic cardboard yet more pleasant. So any project you need to utilize cardboard for can work with the deep cut blade!

Felt sheets – Love felt blooms or crafts? At that point let your Cricut take the necessary steps for you! You can likewise do hardened felt sheets!

Glitter cardstock – I love glitter cardstock for a sort of project. I have cut it with the fine-point cutting edge yet the deep works better particularly with the chunky glitter paper.

Fabric Blade – What Can I Cut?

The fabric blade is entirely explicit to fabric and you will generally keep the fabric setting set up on the dial. Here are a couple of my preferred fabric spots to shop. You can likewise cut fabric with the 2 past blades talked about yet I suggest trying the fabric intended blade a try!

Spoonflower – If you need A LOT of fabric to pick from or to specially craft your very own fabric in a couple of short snaps then Spoonflower is the best approach!

Joann Fabrics – Many of you have most likely known about Joann's Fabrics. They have been around quite a while and some of you may have a store close by. If you don't, you can shop here online!

Fabric Direct – If you need a big website with fabric and at discount costs, at that point make certain to look at fabric direct. I have acquired velvet from them for some fall pumpkin creates and adored it!

Mat to utilize: Fabric grip mat or standard grip.

Knife Blade (Cricut Maker only) – What Can I Cut?

With the knife (Cricut Maker only) you can cut a ton of comparable Cricut materials similarly as with the deep blade BUT the thing that matters is that it can cut 2-3x thicker materials then the Explore can deal with! In fact, the knife blade can slice material up to 3mm thick! All the more significantly, it does it with an increasingly exact and clean accuracy cut then the deep cut blade with Explore.

Mat to utilize: A crisp standard grip mat will work for materials more slender then 1 mm however ordinarily the blade sharp edge is utilized on thicker materials, so I prescribe the solid grip mat. In case you're utilizing something like 3 mm balsa wood you may likewise need to utilize some painter's tape around the edges to ensure it doesn't slide mid-cut.

Settings: For the wood, chipboard, and leather there are settings you can choose with you click on "see all materials" in Design Space. Craft foam typically functions admirably on the thicker cardstock setting.

Rotary Blade (Cricut Maker only) – What Can I cut?

Washi Sheets – Washi Sheets are amazing specialty papers. Typically they have a fabulous time surfaces or prints on them. They work delightfully for cards!

Crepe paper – Can you say simple crepe paper blossoms?

Cork – Cork can be sensitive to cut so the revolving blade is perfect!

Tissue paper – Cut tissue paper with as well! Make a point to pick a greater paper like the one connected here.

Delicate fabrics – Fabrics that are progressively fragile like tulle, organza, and lace are a solid match for the rotary blade.

Mat to utilize: You can utilize a fabric grip mat for light fabrics and cork; however, utilize a standard or light hold tangle for crepe and light for tissue paper.

Settings: Delicate fabrics ought to be set to the fabric selection setting, while the tissue, crepe, and washi paper ought to be put on their named setting inside custom settings.

CHAPTER 7:

Selling and Make Money

In terms of making money from the comfort of your home, you easily achieve that with a Cricut machine. However, you have to bear in mind that there are a number of competitors out there, thus you have to put in extra efforts in order to stand a chance to succeed.

For you to become successful in the Cricut world of crafts, you have to keep the following in mind;

1. Dare to be different

You have to be yourself, unleash your quirkiness and creativity.

Those that have been in the Cricut crafts world for some time know all about the knockout name tiles. They became a hit and in no time, everyone was producing and selling them.

In the crafting world, that is the norm. Thus, you could be among the earliest people to jump on a trend to ride the wave until the following hot seller surfaces. Mind you, that strategy of selling Cricut crafts can become costly and tiresome if you are not careful.

The basic idea here is to add your flair and personal style, and not to completely re-invent the wheel. For example, let's say you come across two name tiles on Etsy, one looks exactly like the other 200+ on sale on the site, while the second one has a few more tweaks and spins on it. The seller of the second product will possibly charge more and accrue a higher profit because his/her product is unique and stands out from the rest.

When you design your products, don't be afraid to tweak your fonts, because even the simplest of tweaks and creativity can make your product stand out from the rest.

Remember this; if you create a product that looks exactly like others, you are only putting yourself in a 'price war', where no one usually wins.

2. Keep it narrow

A lot of crafters out there believe that creating and selling everything under the sun translates into more patronage, and more money, but that isn't how it works. On the contrary, it might only result in a huge stock of unsold products, more burn out and heavy cost. Rather than producing materials here and there, you should focus on being the best in your area of craftiness, so that when people need specific products in your area, they'll come to you.

It can be very tempting to want to spread your tentacles because it might seem like the more you produce, the more options you'll provide for your clients, but that might be counterproductive.

Take out time to think about your area of strength and focus your energy on making products that you'd be known for. It is better to be known as an expert in a particular product than to be renowned for someone that produces a high number of inferior products.

Thus, you should keep it narrow and grow to become the very best in your area of craft.

3. be consistent

If you intend to become successful, you have to work on your Cricut craft business consistently. Some people work once a week or thereabout because they sell as a hobby; however, if you intend to make in-road in your business, you have to work every day.

If you have other engagements and can't work every day, then you should create a weekly schedule and stick to it. If you shun your business for weeks and months at a time, then you will not go anywhere with it.

Apart from consistency in work and production, you also have to be consistent with your product quality and pricing. When your customers are convinced about your products, they will easily recommend you to their friends, family, business partners, and many others.

In business, there are ups and downs, thus, you shouldn't reduce your work rate because things are not going as planned. Success doesn't come easy, but one of the surest ways of being and maintaining success is by consistently doing the things you love.

4. be tenacious

It is not easy to run a business because it involves a lot of hard work, sweat, and even heartbreaks. Thus, you have to bear in mind that there will be days when you will feel like throwing in the towel.

However, you have to look at the bigger picture, because the crafting business is not a get rich quick scheme. Remember, quitters never win, so quitting isn't an option. Keep doing the things you love, and keep improving. Successful people never give up. They suffer many setbacks but they don't stop.

Thus, for you to be successful in your craft, you have to be tenacious and resilient. Be willing to maneuver your way through tough times, and do not forget to pick up lessons.

5. Learn everyday

Be willing to learn from people that have been successful in the business. You don't necessarily have to unravel everything by yourself, because whatever it is you are doing, others have already done it in the past.

Whether you intend to learn how to build a successful Facebook group or how to go up the Etsy ranks, remember that people have already done all that in the past, and are giving out tricks and tips they know.

Make it a tradition to learn something new about your business every day because, at the beginning of your business, you will have to do more marketing than crafting.

When you wake up in the morning, browse through the internet, gather materials and read at your spare time, because the more you learn the better your chances of being successful. They say knowledge is power, and for you to become successful as a craftsman/woman, you have to constantly seek new knowledge in the form of tips, tricks, software upgrades, marketing, design ideas, tools, accessories, and many others.

All I am saying is that you should learn without ceasing.

6. Quality control

If you intend to grow your brand, you must prioritize the selling of high-quality products. Your motto should quality over everything.

For you to easily succeed, people should know you as someone that sells top quality products, because quality wins over quantity every day of the week.

You don't want to be known as someone that produces poor quality items because when the word spreads (and it surely will); your business will pack up.

If you focus your attention and efforts on the production of high-quality materials, you will be able to withstand competition, no matter how stiff it is.

CHAPTER 8:

Cricut Design Space Top Menu

The top menu will only become available after you have texts typed out or a design uploaded. Thus, beginning from the left is the Undo button, used to rectify mistakes. The next button on the right is the Redo button, used to repeat and action.

The Deselect button is next, and it is used as the opposite of select. The Edit button is next and it has a dropdown menu that consists of copy or paste and flip. Next is the Size button; you can use it to change the actual size of your design or explore the bottom right of the design to use the two-way directional arrow.

Right at the bottom left of the canvas is the unlock button. This feature consists of a four-way directional arrow used to widen designs without making them taller or making them taller with making them wider.

On the menu is the rotation tool, used to rotate designs to every degree possible. The last feature on the top menu is the x and y coordinates, used to position designs on the canvas.

How to Weld

It can be a little bit daunting for a Cricut Space beginner to use the weld tool, however, when you become proficient, it'll open the doors to many more projects because it is a tool that will be used often.

The weld tool is located at the bottom right corner of Design Space, under the layers panel. Other tools close to it are; flatten, contour and slice tools.

In Cricut Design Space, the weld tool does the following;

· Connects cursive text and scrip in order for it to cut as a single word instead of individual letters

· Merge multiple layers and shapes into a single layered image

· Take of cut lines from different shapes and cut them as one big image

For you to use weld, the text or shapes you intend to weld together must be touching or overlapping each other.

To select the layers you intend to weld together; select a layer, hold down 'ctrl' and select the other layer. After selecting both layers, click 'weld'. If you intend to weld the whole layers on your canvas, click 'select all' to select all the layers and click 'weld'.

If you weld different layers together, it becomes a single image and will cut out in one color and on one mat.

Without selecting multiple layers, the weld option will not be available for use.

In order to weld texts, you have to make sure that the letters are all touching each other. Thus, you have to reduce the spacing of the letters until they begin to touch each other. Once you do this, you can select everything and click weld.

How to Slice

The slice tool is a feature in Cricut Design Space that cuts one design element out of another. You can use it to cut text from a shape, cut one shape from another shape, or cut overlapping shapes from each other. Below is an example and we will cut text out from a heart shape.

Choose a font

Use any font you prefer, but decrease your letter spacing from to 0.9 so that your letters will link together.

Weld the text

When you're done with the spacing, you have to transform your letters into a single image by using the weld tool. When you weld your letters, it permanently connects all the design elements into one image.

Choose an SVG

You can find a heart SVG from Lovesvg.com. You just need to ungroup everything and simply delete the unwanted elements.

Set the size of your design

You need to resize the image. Depending on the size you want, simply type the intended size on the width box. For this example, we'll stick to 5.5 inches.

Arrange the design

You need to arrange the text and heart, by clicking 'arrange'.

Use the slice tool

When you have arranged your design perfectly, select your text and hold down 'ctrl' key, select the heart and click 'slice'. Now, you can remove the text from the heart and delete.

iii. Once your design is done, it is time to cut vinyl.

How to flatten

The flatten tool is a feature used to turn multi-layered images into a single-layered image.

What does flatten do in Cricut Design Space?

The tool is used in the making of decals, labels, stickers, and much more. You can flatten multiple layers of SVG cut files into single layered images, before printing and cutting.

With the flatten tool, you can achieve the following;

· Remove cut lines from an image

· Transform multi-layered images into a single layered image

- Used to transfer regular images into printable images for print-and-cut
- Used to maintain distinct colors of multi-layered images

Using the flatten tool;

- To select the layers you intend to flatten together, lick 'select all' or hold down 'ctrl' and select the layers
- After selecting, click flatten at the bottom right corner
- When you do that, the image is now flattened.

How to Attach

Basically, there are two distinct reasons for using the attach tool;

- To keep scoring/writing lines in the right place
- To keep shapes in the correct place on the mat as on the canvas

Using the Attach tool to maintain the same arrangement

If you want all the pieces of your project to remain in the exact location during cutting, as it is on your CDS canvas, you have to;

- Select all the items of each color
- Click 'attach' at the lower right corner
- Repeat the process for each color layer until they are all nested under a label that says "attach'

With the attach tool, you will be able to cut out your projects exactly the way you arranged them on your Cricut canvas.

How to Group/Ungroup

Group on Cricut Design Space means to group two or more layers into one layer. On the other hand, Ungroup means breaking up a layer group into separate layers. There are different types of group layers, and if a layer is grouped multiple times, you will have to ungroup them multiple times, in order to separate them completely.

Group: To select multiple layers, you have to press 'ctrl' and select your layers on your computer. After selection, you have to click your mouse right and click the Group button. If you wish, there is also the option of creating multiple groups within groups, because it makes it easier to deal with complex designs.

In Design Space, groups work better with layers, especially when you're trying to manipulate some parts of a design. With Group, you can easily resize or stretch the selection.

Ungroup: It is very easy to ungroup designs that are grouped together. To ungroup, you need to select the layer you intend to ungroup, right click your mouse, and click on the ungroup button or select Ungroup. There are layers that might have been grouped multiple times, thus, if you intend to Ungroup completely, you have to continuously select again and again, and keep clicking Ungroup, until it's completely done.

The primary reason for using the ungroup feature is to change or manipulate some part of a design. The change could be physical, or it could be manipulating some parts of a design by welding, attaching, or using some other methods, without touching on the rest of the design

How to duplicate/delete if you intend to duplicate a layer or set of layers, you have to select the part of the design or the layers you intend to duplicate, right click your mouse and click the Duplicate button.

On the other hand, if you intend to delete a single layer or a set of layers, you have to select the part of the design or the layers you intend to delete, right click your mouse, and select the Delete button.

If you have two designs and you intend to retain only one, select the design you intend to delete, right click your mouse, and click the Delete option.

How to color sync

The reason for such result lies with the fact that you may have used several images from the images tab, all being with slightly different shades of similar colors. In order to overcome this, go up into the top right-hand corner under the green button marked 'Make It'. You will find the option 'Color Sync'. By clicking on it, you will allow the function to pull up every single item on your project to be sorted out by similar color groups.

Here is an example whereby six different shades of green emerge. Consequently, Color Sync will identify six different shades of green, making six different green cutting mats as you make your project. If the final result of your project is to have multiple shades, then there is no need to modify anything. However, if you wish to streamline in order to obtain one green cutting mat, all you have to do is to select items and drag them into different colors. By doing this, you avoid going into each individual layer through a manual change of color. On the other hand, if the purpose is to modify the color in order to obtain one shade, like for instance if you want to put together similar colors to one mat, then select the color shade bar situated on the left-hand side and pull that into the color you want to switch into. This option allows to streamline different colors of cutting mat to only a few. The choice is yours.

Using Text in Cricut Design Space

Once you sign into Cricut Design Space, select one of the three places marked with arrows to start a new project. Then click the three line icon on the top left to proceed for a 'New Project'. As you start a new project, you will be directed to a gridded design space called a Canvas. Select the left sidebar which contains the text icon. A small box will emerge, shown by a second arrow, in which you can enter your text. Once the text entered, chose a font which can be found on the far left arrow. You will quickly notice how the font has large spaces between the letters. To remedy this and bring the letters closer together modify the letter space to a smaller one (negative numbers can also be used to reach the effect needed).

Getting Started with Text

Start typing your text by simply clicking the text icon located on the left toolbar. A text box will appear in which you can start inserting your text. Font, style, and size as wells as line spacing and letter spacing can be selected by going on the top toolbar. It is advisable to type your text first and then make the changes you want afterward.

How to Access Special Characters

You can access special characters by using Humble Scrip which provides many options. You can access it by typing 'character map' in your system search box. The app will appear. A drop-down menu indicates which Font you are working with. Secure the option 'Advanced View' is properly checked. Then modify the Character set to Unicode and finally group by Unicode Subrange. At this stage, a new box will appear for the Unicode Subrange. Scroll it all the way to the bottom and select 'Private Use Characters'.

CHAPTER 9:

Tips and Tricks and Hacks for Cricut Design Space.

1. You Can Customize Make It Now Projects

When you are initial getting started in Design Space, I believe it is best to relieve in and also not attempt to discover whatever at once. Make It Now tasks are tasks that have already been designed, all you have to do is reduced.

To modify Make It Now project, clack on the image of the project you intend to make. It will open up and reveal the materials you need and also instructions. It is a wonderful starting point for your projects and you can customize them to make them your own.

2. You Can Find Even More Ready-Made

If you like the idea of projects that are presently formed, you may wish to have a look at the area in Design Space. Did you know that you can produce a profile and also share your developments? It's a reasonably brand-new attribute, but it is so agreeable to see countless other Cricut users and what they create. They work just like the Make It Now projects, yet they are made by Cricut individuals instead of Cricut themselves.

3. Filter Images

When you prepare to make your very own tasks in Design Space, you will certainly soon understand that there are lots of pictures to pick from! One way that I keep from spending every one of my crafting time scrolling via images is to filter them.

Pictures can be filtered in countless means. The first option is whether you are intending to look for pictures that remain in the cloud or ones that have actually been downloaded to your tool to make use of offline. Following off, you can filter by possession. You can pick all possessions, "my pictures", posted, totally free, Cricut Access, as well as purchased.

You can likewise look for a certain kind of image. The choices to filter by are: any kind of type, 3D appearances, things & backgrounds, boundaries, cards & envelopes, frames phrases as well as. Finally, you can pick the layer kind. You can pick any type of layer, multi-layer or single-layer

As you can picture, searching for a photo that is in the cloud, free, a border and also single-layer will certainly bring up considerably less photos that you would certainly require to browse to find the one that will certainly function just right for your task.

4. Know How to Read the Images

When looking for photos, there are a number of things you may wish to look at. If the image is encompassed in the Cricut Contact registration it will have a little eco-friendly banner and an "an" in the top left corner. Near the bottom in the left edge is the rate, or it will certainly say "bought" if you have actually currently acquired it.

To find extra information click on the "I" in the bottom best corner. A box will turn up that claims that title of the image, the ID number of the photo and the cartridge or set that it is from will be hyperlinked. You may desire to click the web link to the cartridge to see comparable images if you like the style of a picture.

5. Attach.

Among one of the most typical concerns that brand-new Design Space customers experience is when they have everything precisely where they desire them on the Design Space display, yet when they most likely to cut it jumbles every little thing up on the cutting mat.

By default, Design Space will certainly reposition the pictures to take advantage of the products you are utilizing. Then choose affix, if you desire to maintain things spaced precisely as you have them on the screen you require to select all of the photos and also.

6. Creating Fonts.

One of the most effective Design Space tips I can give you is for when you are wanting to create with your Cricut. There is a great deal of irritation when someone goes to complete their task only to see that it simply laid out the font, it didn't really load it in.

Often it is tough to picture what a typeface will look like once it is drawn. The Cricut device's task is to analysis lines, whether it is to reduce them or attract them. You will see precisely where the blade or pen will certainly go if you follow the line however. A lot of typefaces will have internal as well as external lines leaving a space that looks like it requires to be filled out.

The font you pick for composing is very crucial; so vital that Cricut has actually made particular" creating" typefaces. They are font styles that consist of only one line as well as give you the look you want when writing with your Cricut.

7. Slice Only 2 Layers.

The piece function in Design Space permits you to take 2 forms and cut one from the other. I think about it as a cookie cutter. A great deal of disappointment comes when you have actually the pictures picked; however, the piece button is grayed out and won't allow you cut.

The answer is constantly TWO! Anytime this occurs to me I understand that I somehow have more than two layers picked. Also, when I assume I do not, I look in the layers panel and also indeed, I do. Design Space will certainly never let you have more than 2 photos selected when you are slicing.

8. Weld Letters.

When dealing with typefaces, especially manuscripts, you will probably want to connect and WELD the letters.

When you move them where each letter is overlapping the other, you need to WELD. The only way to get letters to produce a single word that is reduced as one item is to overlap the letters and then WELD them.

9. Locate the font name that you used (even bonded).

In some cases, you will wish to know what the typeface is that you utilized, especially if you are returning to a task you currently developed. Design Space will inform you the font style, even if it has been changed into a photo by welding it.

Beneath the symbols at the leading there will be a tiny and it will state "See picture details". Click on that as well as a box will open up that will inform you the chosen typeface.

10. Contour to Hide Parts of an Image.

If there is an image that has parts in it that you don't want, you can remove them! The shape feature enables you to get rid of cut (or creating) lines from a picture.

11. Modification Project Copies # Instead of Copy as well as Paste.

There might be times you need a lot of one photo or more than one whole task cut. You can duplicate as well as paste, however honestly, the easiest means to make more than one of something is to make use of the "project copies" feature instead.

As soon as you have your photo or job ready, proceed as well as send it to cut. In the leading left edge, you can enter in the amount of the job you want and it will instantly place that number on the cutting floor covering.

12. Move as well as Hide Images on Cutting Screen.

In some cases, relocating a cut will assist you conserve much more materials, or you may want to conceal a picture so it won't reduce. Once you get to the cut display, you can rearrange images, move them from one floor covering to another and even conceal them.

Hacks

Wash Your Mats with Soap, Water, and a Gentle Scrubber

Because Cricut strongly encourages you not to clean your mats, it's imperative that you know you're doing this at your own risk. A large number of Cricut craftsmen, however, have said that this little trick has saved them at least for a couple of weeks from having to buy a new mat.

Because Cricut doesn't support any efforts to boost the enduring grip strength on their mats, it's best to stop trying this hack until you're sure you'd need a new mat anyway, so if it doesn't perform well, you can get a new one without feeling like you've lost something.

You can gently clean the adhesive grip side of your mat using warm water (don't go too hot or you might melt the adhesive on your mat) and a mild dish soap like Dawn, Fairy, or Palmolive, and the soft side of a kitchen sponge.

This will ensures that you can use most of the features of the Cricut Design Space. Follow these simple steps and take a look at this selection to clean it well . Then, below, take a look at the best free fonts for Cricut that we have. Make sure you have a Cricut Access membership, and then follow the following steps.

Use Non-Alcohol Wipes to Clean your Mats

Because Cricut strongly encourages you not to clean your mats, it's imperative that you know you're doing this at your own risk. Nonetheless, this hack has been tested by a decent number of people and found it to be a perfect way to give their mats a few extra weeks of life. This is a fundamental step.

Using baby wipes or non-alcohol wipes on your mats can loosen stuff that's caught in your mat's grip, clear away dirt or paper leaves, and can give you a few extra weeks of grip power in your mats!

Don't add too much pressure if you don't want to ground debris any further in, or even scrape the adhesive completely off the surface.

Rinse the mat and pat dry thoroughly with a linen dish towel or a high-quality paper towel that does not leave any residue behind. Schedule the mat to dry completely for an hour or two after you have done so, and then give it a shot to see how much the wash has helped you out.

Doing all these hacks over time should give you an idea of what works, what doesn't, and how much you need to swap your Cricut mats.

Clean your Blades

You can find that your blades are snagging on your materials after some period of continuous use, or that the cuts aren't as sharp as you would light them up to be. If this is the case, remove the housing from its attachment clamp and push the button at the top of the housing. It will stretch the blade beyond the casing, but will also give you a comfortable grip on the blade while you clean it up. Highest priority on the rundown.

CHAPTER 10:

Cricut Design Space Vocabulary

When working with the Cricut cutting machines and Design Space, you are going to come across different terminology. The following is a glossary of the Cricut vocabulary to help you better understands the system. The following are general Cricut terminology as "Design Space" terminology

Backing

Backing is the back sheet of material such as vinyl. It is the part of the material that gets stuck onto the cutting mat and is usually the last part of the material to be removed after cutting, weeding, and transfer of the project.

Bleed

The bleed refers to a space around each item to be cut. This gives the cutting machine the ability to make a more precise cut. It is a small border that separates cutting items on a page. This option can be turned off, but it is not recommended.

Bonded Fabric

Bonded fabric is material that is not very elastic, it is held together with adhesive and is not typical woven type fabric.

If there is some gunk visible on the blade, pinch around the blade shaft using a very careful grip with your opposite thumb and forefinger, and bring it back, making sure you don't go against the blade angle as you do. This will remove any foreign material from your blade tip and make your cuts more accurate.

You may also take a ball of tin foil and poke the blade a few times into the cup, which will remove debris while also allowing a minor sharpening on them.

Blade

Cricut has a few different types of cutting blades and tips. Each blade has its own unique function enabling it to cut various materials.

Blade Housing

The blade housing is the cylindrical tube that holds the blade and fits into the blade head and blade accessory compartment of the Cricut cutting machine.

Blank

Cricut offers items, called blanks, to use with various projects for vinyl, iron-on, heat transfer vinyl, or infusible ink. These items include T-shirts, tote bags, coasters, and baby noisiest.

Brayer

The Brayer is a tool that looks a bit like a lint roller brush. It is used to flatten and stick material or objects down smoothly as it irons out bubbles, creases, etc.

Bright Pad

A Bright Pad is a device that looks like a tablet. This device has a strong backlight to light up materials to help with weeding and defining intricate cuts. It is a very handy tool to have and can be used for other DIY projects as well.

Butcher Paper

Butcher paper is the white paper that comes with the Cricut Infusible Inks sheets. It is used to act as a barrier between the EasyPress or iron when transferring the ink sheet onto a blank or item.

Carriage

The carriage is the bar in the Cricut cutting machine which the blade moves across.

Cartridge

Cartridges are what the older models of the Cricut cutting machine used to cut images. Each cartridge would hold a set of images. They can still be used with the Cricut Explore Air 2 which has a docking site for them. If you want to use them with a Cricut Maker you will have to buy the USB adaptor. Design Space still supports the use of Cartridge images.

Cartridges also come in a digital format.

Cricut Maker Adaptive Tool System

The Cricut Maker comes with an advanced tools system control using intricate brass gears. These new tools have been designed to aid the machine in making precise cuts and being able to cut more materials such as wood, metal, and leather.

Cut Lines

These are the lines along which the cutting machine will cut out the project's shapes.

Cutting Mat

There are a few different types of cutting mats also known as machine mats. Most of the large mats can be used on both the Cricut Explore Air 2 and the Cricut Maker. The Cricut Joy needs mats that are designed specifically for it.

Cut Screen

When you are creating projects in Design Space, there is a green button on the top right-hand corner of the screen called the Make it button. When the project is ready to be cut, this button is clicked on. Once that button has been clicked, the user is taken to another screen where they will see how the project is going to be cut out. This is the Cut Screen.

Drive Housing

The Drive Housing is different from the Blade Housing in that it has a gold wheel at the top of the blade. These blades can only be used with the Cricut Maker cutting machine.

EasyPress

A Cricut EasyPress is a handheld pressing iron that is used for iron-on, heat transfer vinyl (HTV), and infusible ink. The EasyPress' latest models are the EasyPress 2 and the EasyPress Mini.

EasyPress Mat

There are a few different EasyPress Mat sizes that are available on the market. These mats make transferring iron-on, heat transfer vinyl, and infusible ink a lot simpler. These mats should be used for these applications instead of an ironing board to ensure the project's success.

Firmware

Firmware is a software patch, update, or new added functionality for a device. For cutting machines it would be new driver's updates, cutting functionality, and so on.

Both Design Space software, Cricut cutting machines, and Cricut EasyPress 2 machines need to have their Firmware updated on a regular basis.

Go Button

This can also be called the "Cut" button. This is the button on the Cricut cutting or EasyPress machine that has the green Cricut "C" on it. It is the button that is pressed when a project is ready to be cut or pressed for the EasyPress models.

JPG File

A JPG file is a common form of digital image. These image files can be uploaded for use with a Design Space project.

Kiss Cut

When the cutting machine cuts through the material but not the material backing sheet it is called a Kiss Cut.

Libraries

Libraries are lists of images, fonts, or projects that have been uploaded by the user or maintained by Cricut Design Space.

PNG File

A PNG file is another form of a graphics (image) file. It is most commonly used in Web-based graphics for line drawings, small graphic/icon images, and text.

Ready to Make Projects

Design Space contains ready to make projects which are projects that have already been designed. All the user has to do is choose the project to load in Design Space, get the material ready, and then make it to cut the design out. These projects can be customized as well.

Scraper Tool

The Scraper tool comes in small and large. It is used to make sure material sticks firmly to a cutting mat, object, or transfer sheet.

Self-Healing Mat

Cricut has many handy accessories and tools to help with a person's crafting. One of these handy tools is the Self-Healing Mat. This mat is not for use in a cutting machine but can be used with handheld slicing tools to cut material to exact specifications

SVG File

The SVG file format is the most common format for graphic files in Cricut Design Space. This is because these files can be manipulated without losing their quality.

Transfer Sheet/Paper

A transfer sheet or transfer paper is a sheet that is usually clear and has a sticky side. These sheets are used to transfer various materials like transfer vinyl, sticker sheets, and so on onto an item.

Weeding/Reverse Weeding

Weeding is the process of removing vinyl or material from a cut pattern or design that has been left behind after removing the excess material. For example, weeding the middle of the letter "O" to leave the middle of it hollow.

Reverse Weeding would be leaving the middle of the letter "O" behind and removing the outside of it.

Weeding Tool

The Weeding tool has a small hooked head with a sharp point. This tool is used to pick off the material that is not needed on a cut. For instance, when cutting out the letter 'O' the weeding tool is used to remove the middle of the letter so that it is hollow. Cleaning up a cut design with the Weeding tool is called weeding.

CHAPTER 11:

How to Edit and Upload Images in The Cricut Machine

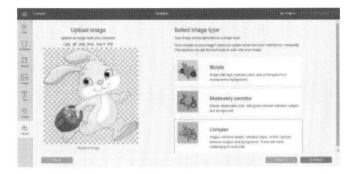

First, you will need to browse the image on your computer and upload it using the "Upload" command. After that, you will want to choose, from the three image options, the "Complex" type. Once you have done all that just select "Continue".

In the next part, you will be taken to a window with various editing options. You will have the option Undo/Redo any action or Zoom in/Zoom out from the image (1). On the left side you will have the most important tools for this job: "Select & erase", "Erase" and "Crop" (2). In this example, we will be using all three of these tools so you can get the full set of information from this technique. First, we will separate the basket from the rabbit and after that, we will separate the rabbit from the basket.

Step 1: If necessary zoom out to be able to view the entire picture.

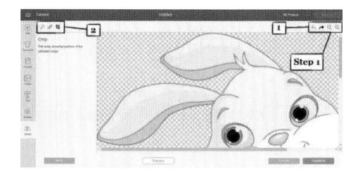

Step 2: If you want to separate a small part of a larger picture, use the "Crop" tool to isolate the targeted area. In this case, we need only the basket so most of the image can be cropped out.

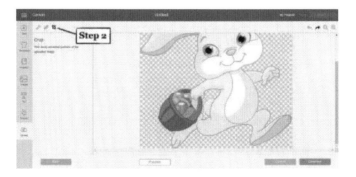

Step 3: Once the rest of the image is cropped we need to remove any part of the remaining picture that we don't want. To do that we can use the "Select & erase" tool.

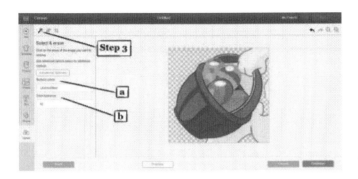

By selecting "Advanced Options" you can directly remove the color by using the "Reduce colors" tab (a). You can also increase the "Color tolerance" (b) which allows you to clear large portions more easily with the "select" method.

Step 4: To remove the fine lines and small details we can use the "Erase" tool.

Tip: Depending on your image you can increase or decrease the size of the eraser by moving the slider left or right.

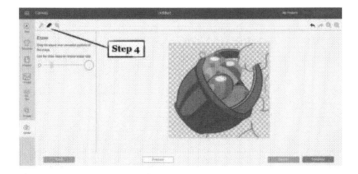

Step 5: Click "Continue" button.

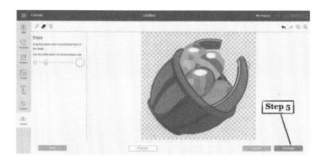

Step 6: Select the type of image that you want to save and click "Save". Here you can choose between a "Print then cut image" or "Cut image".

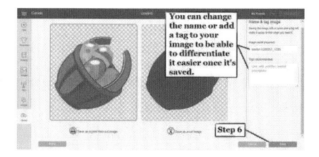

Step 7: Once we have our first part separated (the basket) we can move on to the rabbit. To do that we need to upload the image again and repeat the process.

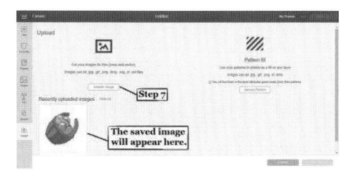

Step 8: Follow the same steps as before but now remove the basket using the "Select & erase" and the "Erase" tool again.

Step 9: Once the image is saved we can add our separated pictures on our canvas. To do that you have first to select each image and then use the "Insert Images" button.

Result: Each image is now considered as its own layer and can be resized, moved and edited to your liking.

Knockout Text Method

You've probably heard about this method or read about it on different forums. However, this method is only limited by your imagination and as your skills progress you will quickly realize that it can be used in multiple ways to enhance your projects.

In this example, we will use it on a text object and by the end of it, you will learn how to add a personalized twist to any text you want.

Step 1: Write your text on the canvas.

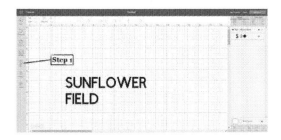

Step 2: This part is very important. Here we will edit the text in such a way that will allow the editing to be visible. You have to choose a font with thick letters. After that, you can change the spacing between the letters and the text rows. Depending on your design you might want to make sure that the letters won't touch each other. But this can vary from project to project.

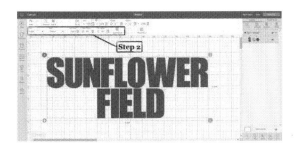

Step 3: Once you are satisfied with your text you can begin adding images that will later be embedded into the final design. In this step, you can let your creativity shine. You can choose images that will be added to single letters or images that will be spread across multiple letters. Chose whatever you think fits best.

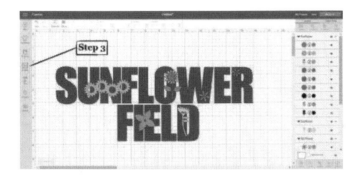

Step 4: Since the images contain multiple layers, they have to be welded together. That is why you have to select all images, except the text, and use the "Weld" tool.

Tip: Even if you add a single image, if that image contains multiple layers, it still has to be welded so you can continue with this method.

Step 5: Once the images are welded together, select both remaining objects (text and welded image) and use the "Slice" tool.

Step 6: Don't be alarmed if after the "Slice" the result will look confusing. In this part, it's best first to select the sliced text and move it to the back of the canvas. That way you will know not to delete that layer.

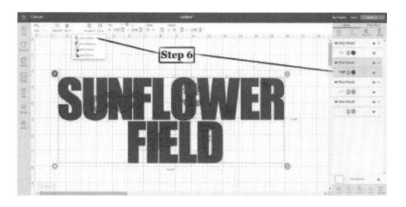

Step 7: All that remained now is to delete the extra objects that resulted after the "Slice".

Tip: You can use the on/off visibility option (eye symbol) for each layer to see if it actually has to be deleted or not.

Result: As you can see in the final image the flower objects are now part of the text and the extra parts have been removed from the canvas.

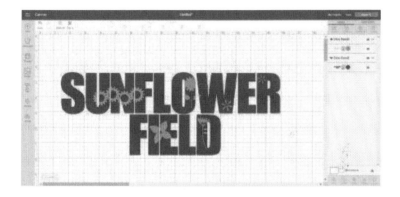

This was just an example to illustrate how you can learn to use the "knockout" method. It's worth mentioning that this method is extremely versatile and can be used to create a lot of different designs. Depending on your style and imagination you can adapt it and let your creativity run free.

In the next image, you can see a few more examples of this method.

Add Color to an Uploaded Image Outline

This method might seem a bit tricky at the beginning since it has a lot of steps. However, the idea is very simple, once you understand the concept you will be able to master it pretty quickly.

Step 1: Upload your image. It should have a clear and defined outline. Also, note that the more complex the image the more work you'll have to do to color each part. But more on that later.

Step 2: Select the image type as "Complex" and click "Continue".

Step 3: If your image is not a .png file it will have a white background. For this method to work, you'll have to remove that background by using the "Select & erase" tool.

Step 4: Once you removed the background you should be left only with the outline of your picture.

Step 5: Select the type of the image to be and click "Continue". For this example, we saved it as a "Cut" image.

Step 6: After the image is uploaded and saved, add it to your canvas.

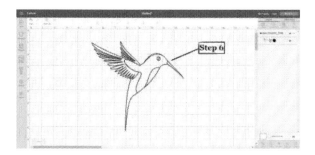

Step 7: In this step, you want to copy and paste your image. You can do that by using the combinations on your keyboard Ctrl + C and Ctrl + V. It's important not to use the duplicate function since it will not save the image in the system's memory. This will be important later on.

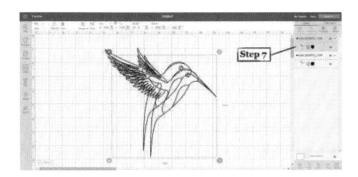

Step 8: Select both images and use the "Align" (Center) tool.

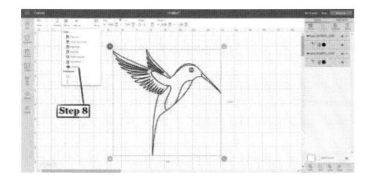

Step 9: Select the lowest image on the Layers tab and use the "Contour" tool.

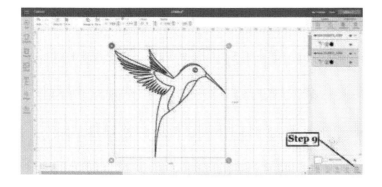

Step 10: This step is very important since from this window you will be selecting the part of the image you want to fill. To make it easier, here is a strategy you can follow for this step:

1. In the bottom right corner select "Hide All Contours".

2. Click somewhere outside the outer border of your image.

This way you will be left with the inside contour you want to color.

Step 11: Select the new image, that should be the inside contour and change it to the desired color.

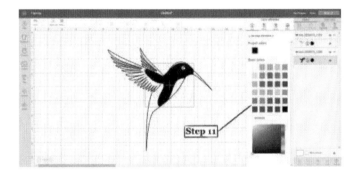

Step 12: For the method to go smoothly from here now on it's better if the images are grouped together. Therefore, you should select both images and use the "Group" command.

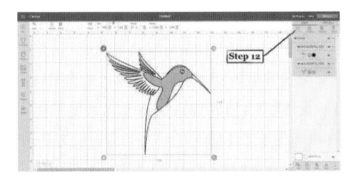

Step 13: If you used the Copy + Paste method, in the beginning, you can now just press Ctrl + V and paste another image outline.

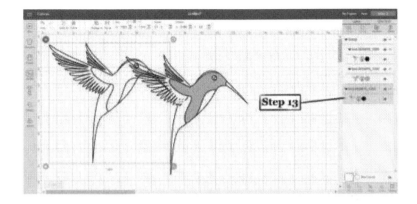

Step 14: Since our initial images are grouped they can now be easily aligned with the newly added image outline. Select the group and the new image and use the "Align" (Center) tool.

Step 15: Once the images are aligned select the lowest image on the layers tab and use the "Contour" tool again.

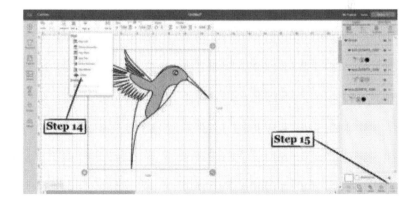

Step 16: Right now, you want to select another part of the image you want to fill. You can use the strategy from Step 10.

Step 17: Once you colored another part of the image you need to "Ungroup" the first group. That way you can avoid having a group within a group within a group later on.

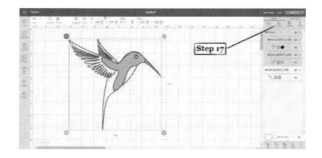

Step 18: Once all layers are ungrouped you can now use the "Group" tool on all existing layers.

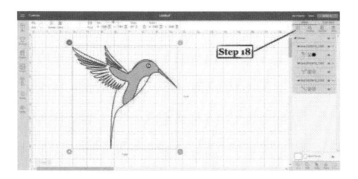

Step 19: From now on you can just repeat Steps 13-18 until you filled every part of your image.

Result: The result should be a fully colored image with a separate layer for each area.

CHAPTER 12:

Slice, Flatten, Weld, Attach and Contour Info-Graphic Slice

The slice tool is ideal for cutting out distinct forms, text, and other elements. When I chose both shapes and clicked on slice, you will see that all the original files will be cut up; to show you what the final result was, I pasted the "slice result" and then divided all the parts resulting from slicing.

Weld

The welding tool combines two or more forms in one. When I have clicked on Weld and chosen both shapes, you can see I formed a new shape. The back layer determines the color, so the original shape is pink in color.

Attach

Attach operates like grouping layers, but firm. When I have chosen both forms and clicked on attach, you will see the layers just changed color. The forms are linked, however, and this attachment will stay in location after I send my project to be cut.

Flatten

This tool supports the Print and then Cut Fill environment; if you alter the fill from no fill to print, it only applies to one layer. However, what if you want to do various forms at the moment?

When your design is finished, pick the layers you want to print together as a whole, then click on flatten. When completing your design, pick the layers you want to print together as a whole, then click on flatten.

In such case, the element becomes a print then cut design, and that's why it no longer shows a black edge through which the blade passes.

Contour

The Contour tool enables you to conceal unwanted parts of a design and will only be allowed if a model or shape has elements that can be left out.

For this instance, I combined the initial design in one form with the weld tool; then I wrote the term contour and cut it against the new form, using the Contour tool to conceal the two letters O's inner circles and the letter R's inner part.

Color Sync

Color Sync is the last panel choice.

Every color on your canvas is a different material color. If your structure has various colors of yellows or blues, do you need them? If you only need one yellow shade, like this instance. Just click and drag the tone to get rid of and drop it on the one you want to maintain.

Cricut Design Space Canvas Area

Canvas Area

There you see all your designs and elements. It's intuitive and user-friendly.

a. Canvas Grid and measurements

The area of the canvas is separated by a grid; this is good because every little square you see on the grid helps visualize the cutting mat. Ultimately, this helps maximize your room. You can alter the readings from cm to inches by clicking the top panel toggle and then selecting Settings. A window will open with all choices.

Design Space Settings

Turning off-grid and turning off-grid and

b. Selection whenever you select one or more layers, the choice is blue and can be modified from all four angles.

The "redx" deletes the layers. The upper right hand corner allows you to rotate the picture (if you need a particular angle, I suggest using the editing menu tool). The selection's reduced right button, "the tiny lock," keeps size proportional when increasing or decreasing your layer size. By clicking, you can now have distinct proportions.

c. Last but not least, zoom in and out. If you want to see in a smaller or larger scale without modifying the original size of your designs, then you can do it by pressing"+ and-" signs on the canvas' lower-left corner. That's it— you're no longer a beginner.

Conclusion

Thank you for reading this manuscript. The following step is to utilize your new found wisdom on the cutting edge craft project designing and creation offered by "Cricut". You are now poised to follow the detailed instructions described in this manuscript to create your own personalized and one of a kind craft projects that reflect your creativity and serve as an exhibit of yourself expression. The possibilities that the Cricut machine has to offer are endless. Every craftsman, beginner, or professional creates beautiful craft pieces according to their level of expertise regarding the Cricut Machine, and after reading this manuscript, you will not be left out. This manuscript has deliberated enough information that you are already ready to go and perform a great artwork of which the world will be proud. So get to work straight away and start creating beautiful crafts. Owning this type of machine is a prime opportunity for many people to develop their expertise in craftsmanship, and it's incredible if you want to venture out and try new things as a crafter because you can add so many new items to your portfolio.

As a result, this machine can literally offer never-ending opportunities for a crafter. In this manuscript, we've discussed how to set up your Cricut machine as well as the advantages of owning one, and we gave you all the information you need to be able to use it efficiently and effectively. It is very typical to get overwhelmed when you own a

Cricut machine because of all the information. Still, we told you exactly what you need to know to get started and start creating impressive and innovative projects. There's so much information out there, and the best part is that most of it is free, which means you have more opportunities to get images and things you need to craft, but it also means you get a much bigger chance to get ideas for your projects. Most people don't even know where to get information about their machine or the items they can use to start crafting, but this manuscript has all the information you need from describing the Cricut machine's most basic function to reflecting ideas for experienced users. We have also shown you that once you have the required skills and the right resources, you can cut even more with the Cricut machines, so you are aware of this as well. In this way, we've made sure you can never forget exactly what you can cut using this machine. However, if you're ever confused, there's a whole part in this manuscript on how to set up your machine and how to set up your design space. We have also included some helpful hints and tips to make sure you have some great ideas on how to make it easier for you to use this machine and the supplies, and you can use all of these tips to your advantage. If you follow the tips you've found in this manuscript, you're going to be able to find supplies easier, keep your mats cleaner, use your machine way better, maintain your machine considerably better, and even gain some amazing storage tips and actually make your craft space a place you can be proud of and feel happy and content while you're working. The ability to do that will help boost both your craftsmanship and your emotions.

Manufactured by Amazon.ca
Bolton, ON